RAY'S BIG DAY

A Journey at the Speed of Light

Josh Lewis

Orchard Books
an imprint of Scholastic Inc.
New York

In a flash,
Ray shot out from the **SUN**.

Glowing with excitement, Ray sped off to see the solar system.

She zoomed past
MERCURY, ***VENUS***, ***EARTH***, and ***MARS*** —
four planets in just minutes.

Next, Ray entered the **ASTEROID BELT**,
zipping past thousands of asteroids and the dwarf planet **CERES**.

Then Ray jetted past ***JUPITER.***

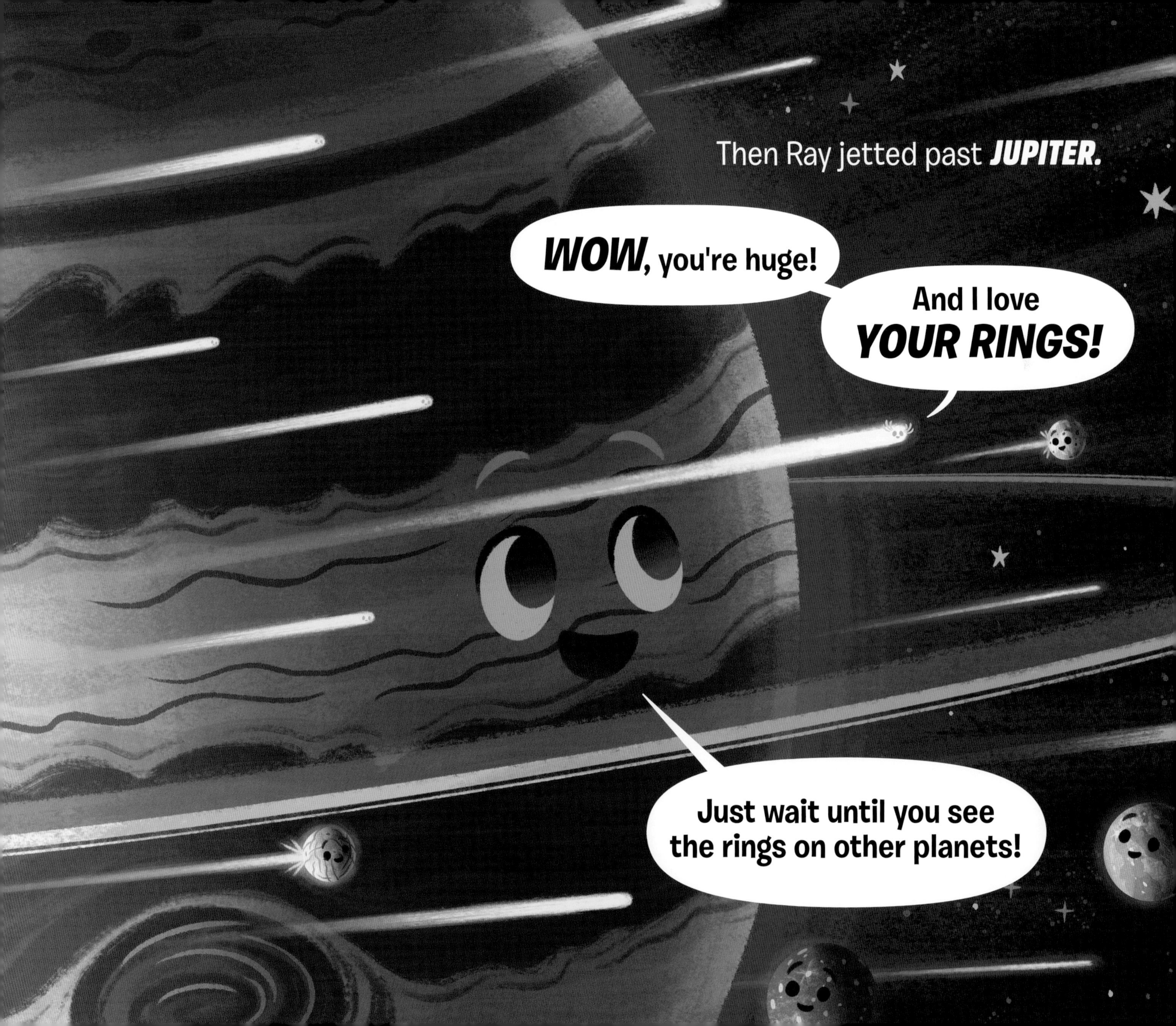

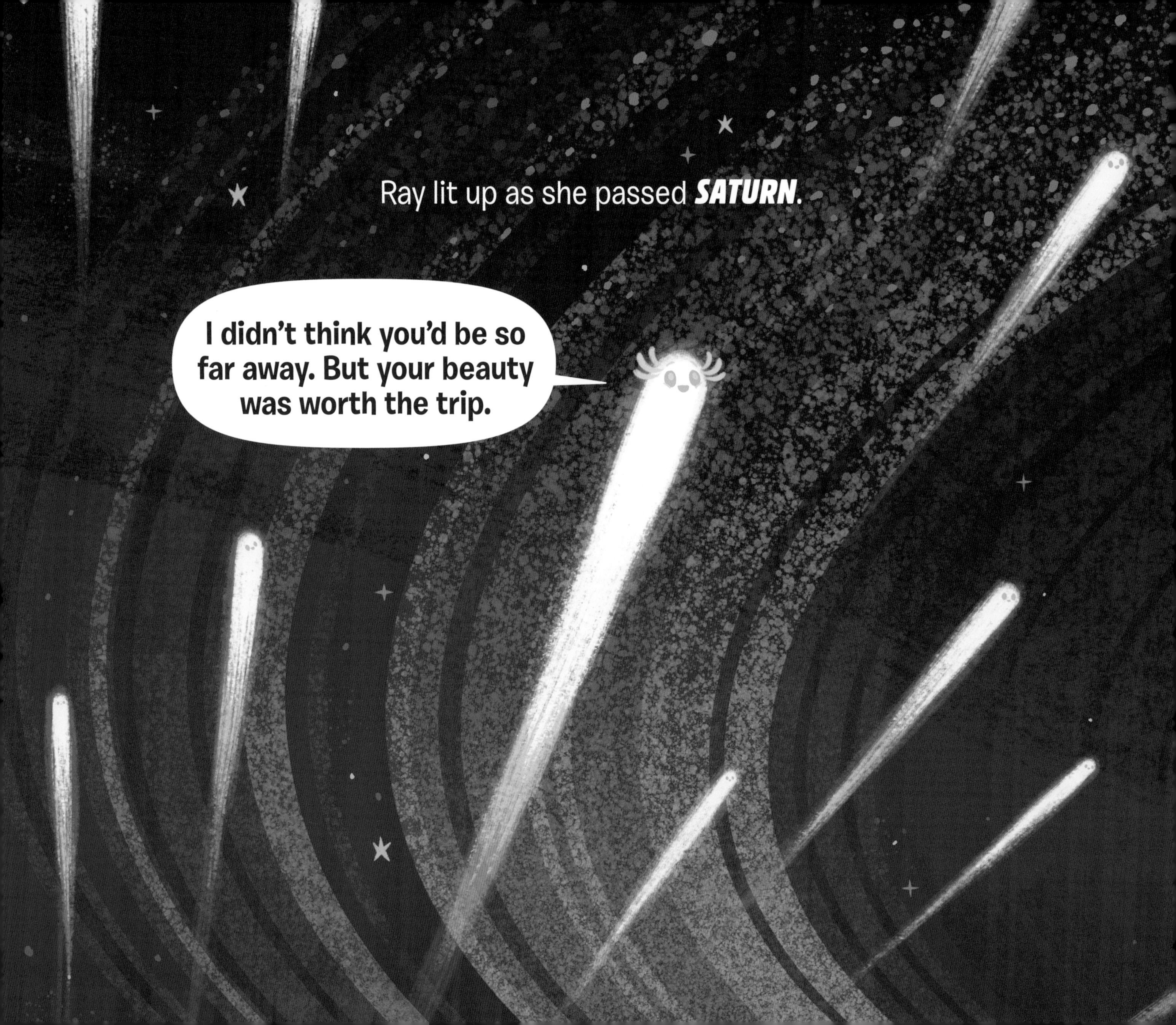

Ray lit up as she passed ***SATURN***.

After waiting and waiting,
Ray whooshed past **_URANUS_**.

Ray zoomed patiently
until she found ***NEPTUNE***.

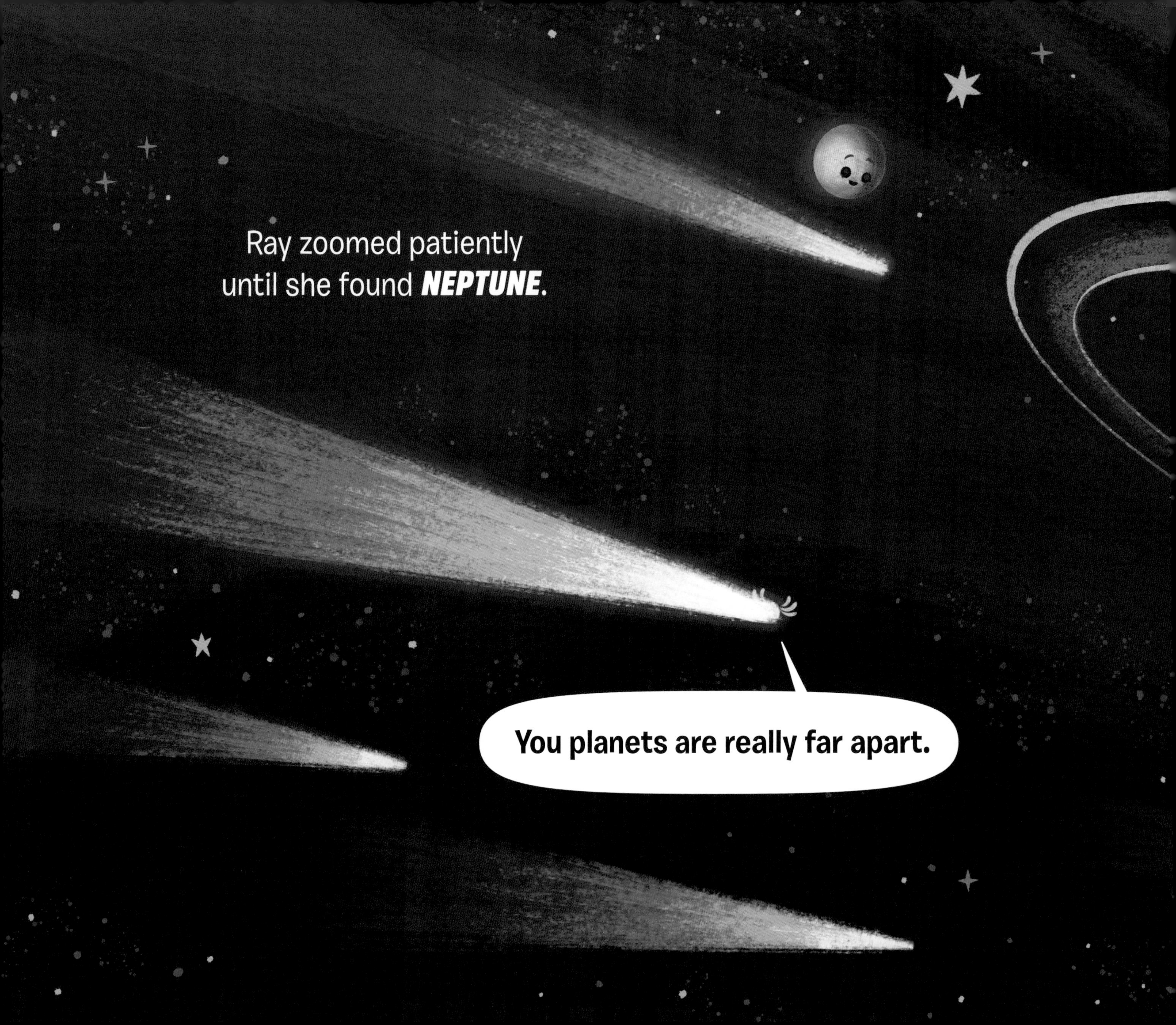

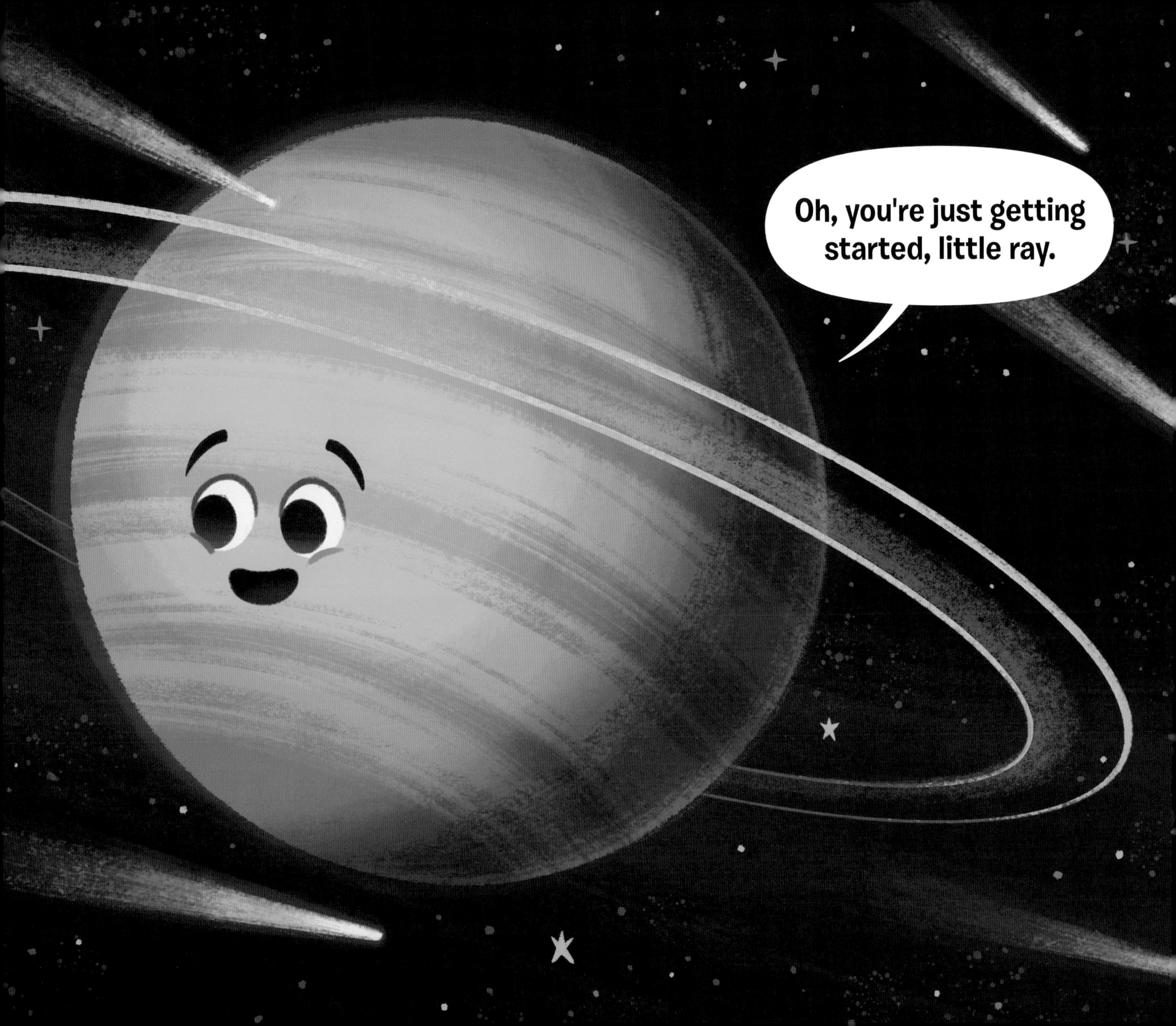
Oh, you're just getting started, little ray.

In almost no time, Ray reached the **KUIPER BELT**.

HEY, RAY!

There was so much to see — thousands
of comets with dwarf planets
PLUTO, HAUMEA, and **MAKEMAKE**
sprinkled in between.

Ray passed them all ...

But she quickly found herself alone.

Worried there was nothing left to see,
Ray tried thinking of something —
anything — to do!

She made up her own theme song . . .

Then she counted as
high as she could.

1 zillion and 1

1 bajillion and 2

1 katrillion and 3

She tried speeding up,
but that didn't work.

She tried turning left,
then right, but she couldn't
change directions.

So she just stared
out into space.

Ray drifted in the darkness for hours until . . .

She reached the dwarf planet **ERIS** and its sidekick moon.

I didn't think anyone else was out here. Are you all that's left?

WHY, HEAVENS NO!
Countless galaxies are ahead of you. Each one is filled with millions of stars, planets, black holes — it's all too vast for anyone to see in a lifetime.

SO ENJOY YOUR JOURNEY!

Ray immediately felt brighter!

As she looked out into the universe
again, she noticed something new.
She was surrounded by twinkling stars!

PRETTY!

There must be a
bazillion of them!

Then a brilliant idea hit her!

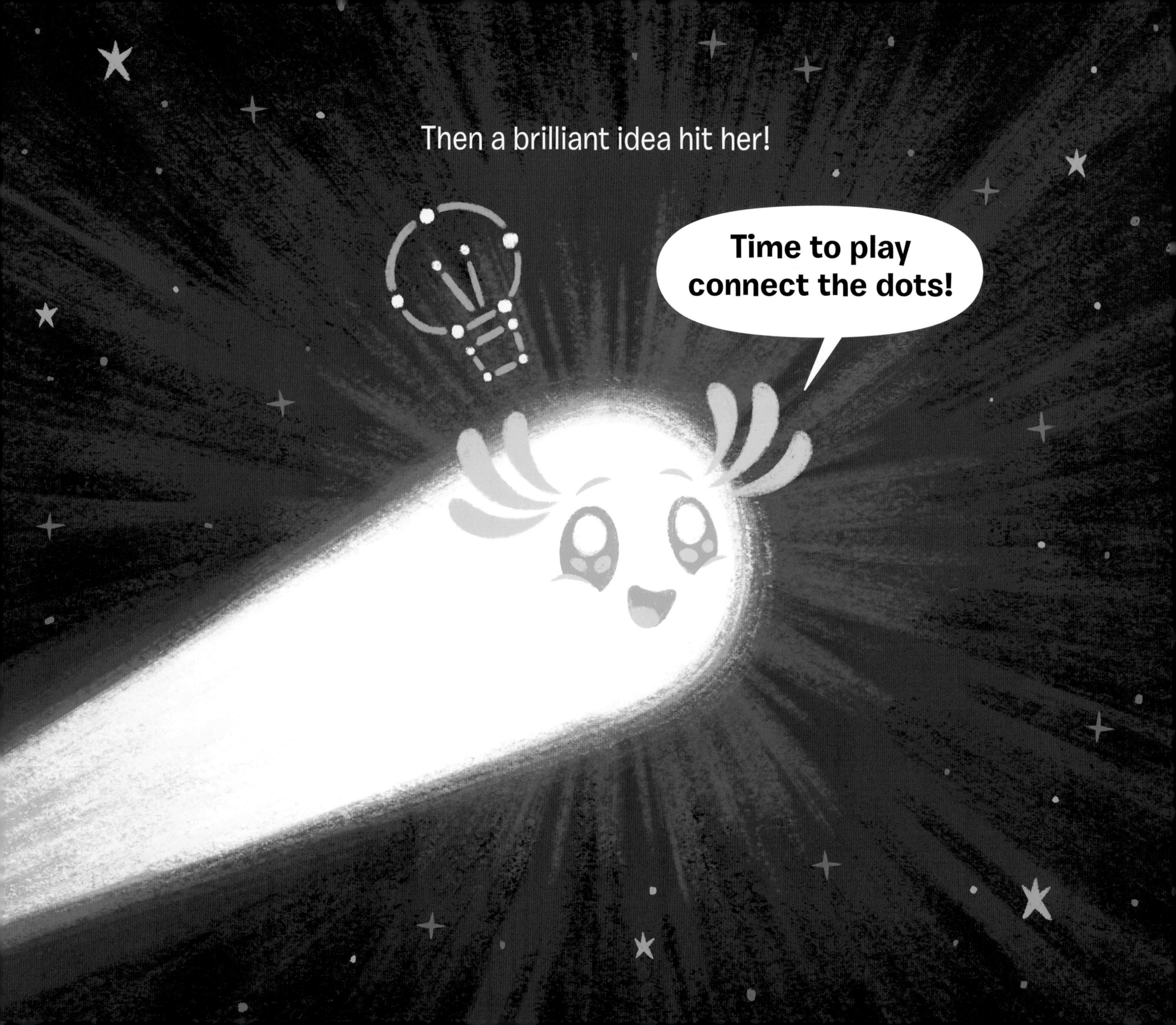

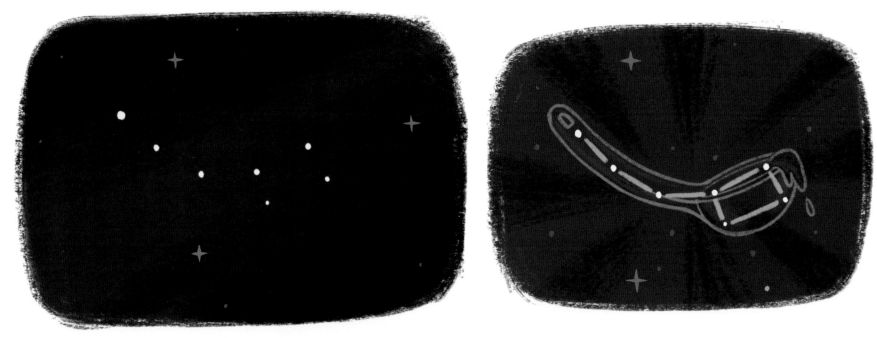

Ray drew a little dipper here . . .

And a bear there. This was fun . . . really, really fun!

For hours and hours,
Ray connected the twinkling dots.
She made . . .

a lion,

a crab,

a dog,

a horse with wings,

a dragon chasing a king,

and hundreds more. She called them constellations.

Before she knew it, Ray had filled
the empty space with creations all her own.
And the entire solar system marveled!

Is that a sea monster?!

Each kind word caused Ray to shine even brighter. She beamed with pride and wondered . . .

Glowing with excitement,
Ray sped off to illuminate
the universe.

AT THE SPEED OF LIGHT

Stars, like our sun, create lots and lots of little rays of light every second. Even though light is the fastest thing there is, it still takes light a very long time to travel through space.

Light travels at about

186,000
miles per second

Planet Distances

SUN · MERCURY · VENUS · EARTH · MARS · CERES · ASTEROID BELT · JUPITER · SATURN

How much time did it take Ray to reach each planet?

⏱ Time from the sun

📏 Average distance from the sun

Rocky Planets
Orbiting closest to the sun, these planets are all made of rocks.

MERCURY
⏱ **3 min 13 sec**
📏 36,000,000 miles

VENUS
⏱ **6 min**
📏 67,000,000 miles

EARTH
⏱ **8 min 19 sec**
📏 93,000,000 miles

MARS
⏱ **12 min 40 sec**
📏 142,000,000 miles

Ray could travel around Earth
7.5 TIMES IN 1 SECOND.

CERES (seer-eez)
⏱ **22 min 58 sec**
📏 257,000,000 miles

URANUS · NEPTUNE

Gas Giants

You can't stand on these super-big planets because they are made of clouds. Each one has a ring system and lots of moons!

JUPITER
⏱ **43 min 17 sec**
📏 484,000,000 miles

SATURN
⏱ **1 hr 19 min**
📏 886,000,000 miles

URANUS
⏱ **2 hr 39 min**
📏 1,784,000,000 miles

NEPTUNE
⏱ **4 hr 10 min**
📏 2,795,000,000 miles

Dwarf Planets

All of these tiny planets are smaller than Earth's moon and have low gravity.

PLUTO
⏱ **5 hr 28 min**
📏 3,670,000,000 miles

HAUMEA (haw-me-uh)
⏱ **5 hr 59 min**
📏 4,010,000,000 miles

MAKEMAKE (maw-kee-maw-kee)
⏱ **6 hr 17 min**
📏 4,215,000,000 miles

ERIS (air-es)
⏱ **9 hr 26 min**
📏 6,289,000,000 miles

How far did Ray travel in one day?

RAY ⏱ **24 hr**
📏 16,104,000,000 miles

Our solar system covers billions of miles of space! So it's very hard to show its true size. The distances between planets are shown to scale.

PLUTO   HAUMEA   MAKEMAKE

ERIS

KUIPER BELT

HORSEHEAD NEBULA

1,375 light-years from Earth

**For Micah, Hannah, and James.
Enjoy your journey!**

ISBN 978-1-339-01734-1

10 9 8 7 6 5 4 3 2 1   24 25 26 27 28

Printed in China   38
First edition, July 2024

Book design by Doan Buu.
The text type was set in Burbank Small.
The display type was hand-lettered.

The illustrations were created in Procreate with digital gouache brushes by Retro Supply Co. and Max Ulichney.